My Truck

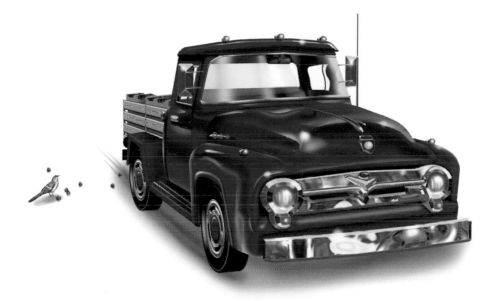

Rebecca Sabatani

Illustrated by Gaston Vanzet

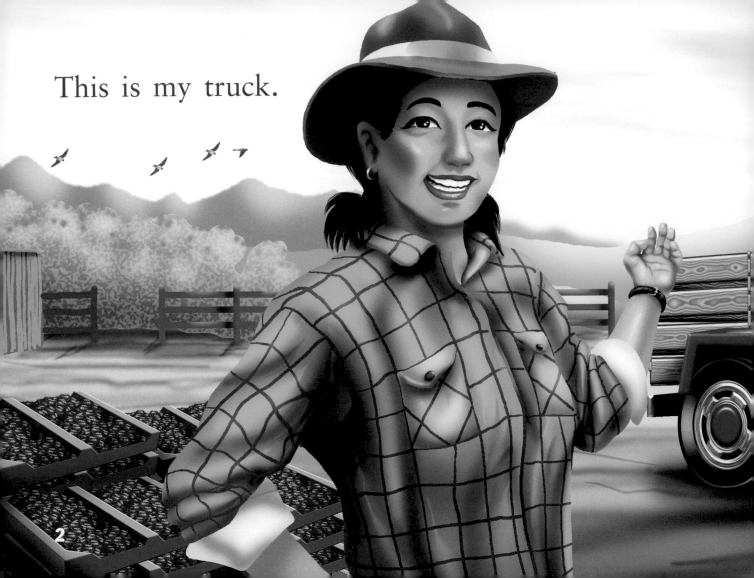

This is my truck.

2

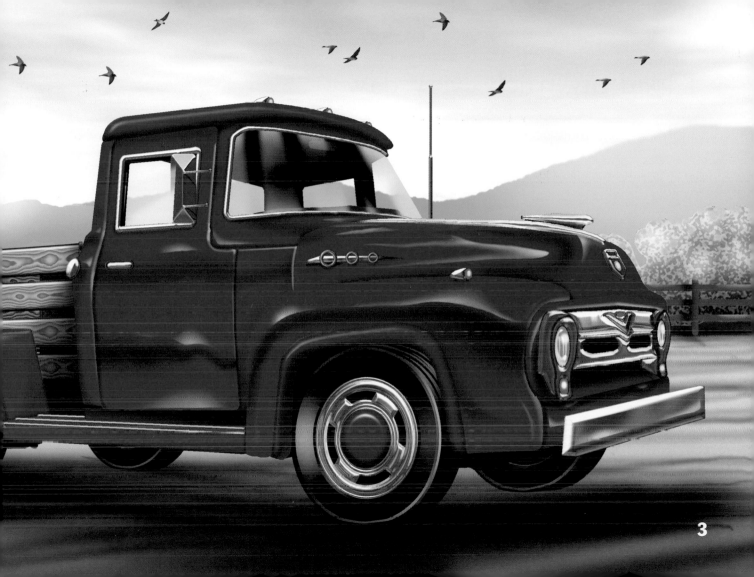

I load my truck every day.

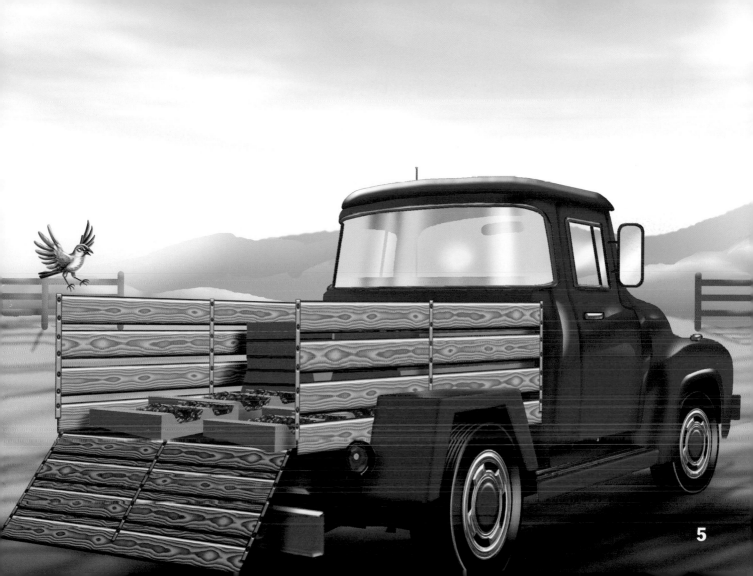

I drive my truck every day.

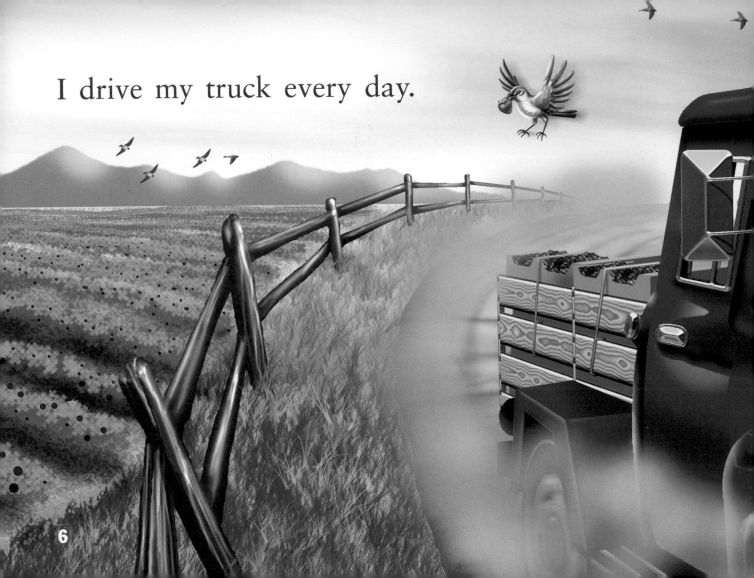

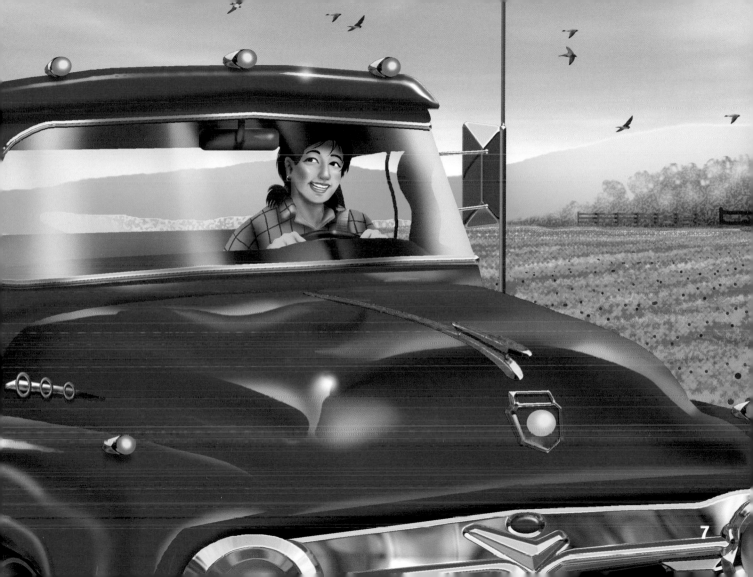

I unload my truck every day.

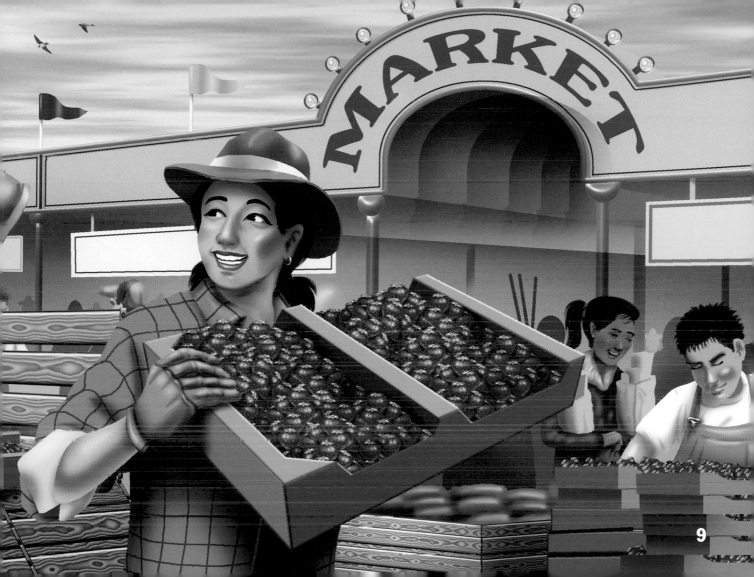

I clean my truck every day.

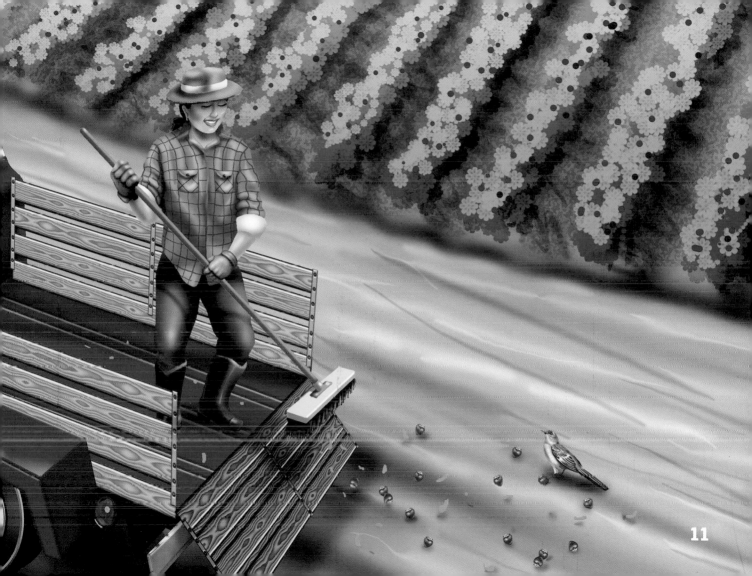

I like my truck!

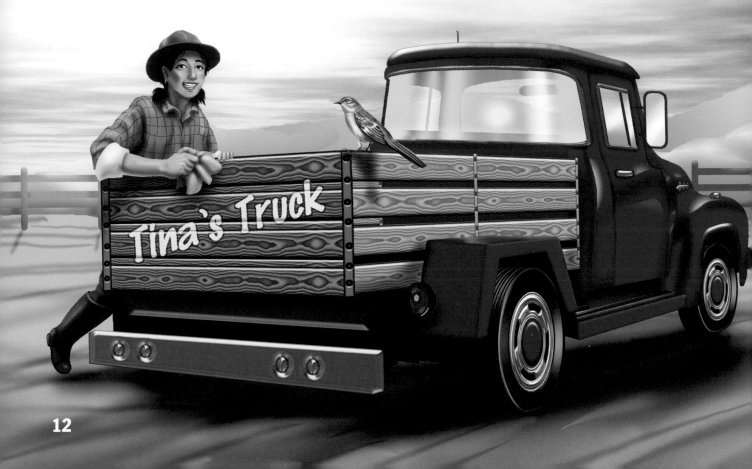

Tina's Truck